FAMOUS PEOPLE GREAT EVENTS

Anne Frank

By Harriet Castor
Illustrated by Helena Owen

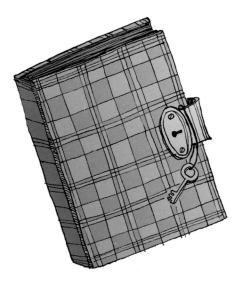

W

FRANKLIN WATTS

This edition 2012

Franklin Watts
338 Euston Road
London NW1 3BH

Franklin Watts Australia
Level 17/207 Kent Street
Sydney NSW 2000

Text first published as *Famous People, Famous Lives:*
Anne Frank in 1996

ISBN: 978 1 4451 0865 0

A CIP catalogue record for this book
is available from the British Library.

Dewey Decimal Classification Number: 40.5'318'092

Series editor: Sarah Peutrill
Original series editor: Sarah Ridley
Artwork: Helena Owen (line), Rory Walker (colour)

Consultants: Dr Anne Millard and David Wray

We thank the Anne Frank Foundation in Basle,
Switzerland, for the basic rights.
Printed in China

Franklin Watts is a division of Hachette Children's Books,
an Hachette UK company.
www.hachette.co.uk

Chapter 1

Anne Frank lived with her parents, her older sister Margot, and their cat in a flat in Amsterdam, in the Netherlands.

Anne was bright and chatty, with lots of friends.

Anne and her family were German – and they were Jewish, too. They had left Germany when it was taken over by a man called Adolf Hitler and his followers, the Nazis.

Hitler hated Jews and wanted to kill them all.

In June 1942, Anne had
her thirteenth birthday.

She got a jigsaw puzzle,
a brooch, some books and
some sweets.

But the best present of all was
a diary. Anne had never had one
before. She was delighted!

Anne started writing in her diary.
She made up a friend called 'Kitty',
and wrote letters to her, describing
her happy life in Amsterdam.

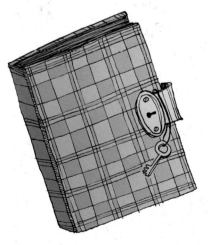

Anne carried on writing to Kitty for the next two years, but during that time her life changed a great deal.

Chapter 2

It was wartime. Hitler had sent his army
to invade other countries in Europe. People
fought against them but the Germans carried
on. When they invaded the Netherlands,
life soon became very difficult for the Jewish
people there.

Hitler made lots of laws against Jews. They had to wear yellow stars. They couldn't have jobs. They weren't allowed bicycles or cars. They couldn't go out after eight o'clock at night, even just to sit in their own gardens.

Then the Nazis started taking
Jews away to terrible places,
called concentration camps,
and a letter came to the Franks'
flat saying that they wanted to
take Margot.

Anne's parents didn't want
Margot to go. They were afraid
of what would happen to her.

They decided the whole family had to hide from the Nazis.

Where shall we hide?

Don't worry – everything's arranged.

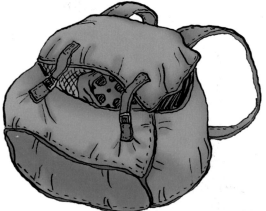

Anne couldn't take a suitcase in case the Nazis got suspicious.

So she packed a few belongings in her satchel, and put on as many clothes as she could.

She wore a dress, a skirt, a jacket, some shorts, three pairs of pants, two vests and much more!

Then Anne's family went to live in the hiding place.

Phew!

Chapter 3

Mr Frank had prepared some rooms in the building where he used to work. They were at the back, upstairs. The entrance to them was hidden behind a bookcase.

In her diary, Anne called the place the Secret Annex.

Keeping the Annex a secret was very important, so Mr Frank told only a few of the office workers about it. They promised to help.

One of them was Miep Gies. Miep brought the Franks food, books and news from the outside world.

Life in the Annex was strange. Anne described it in her diary.

During the day, when there were office workers downstairs, the Franks had to be very quiet. They couldn't flush a toilet or run a tap until the workers went home for the night.

The Annex

The office

Anne found it hard having to be quiet all the time. She longed to go outside, and laugh and play in the sunshine.

Anne often quarrelled with her mother and Margot. Sometimes she felt her diary was her only good friend.

Chapter 4

Soon, another Jewish family came to hide with the Franks: Mr and Mrs van Pels and their son, Peter. Later an eighth person joined them: a dentist called Mr Pfeffer.

Anne had to share a room with Mr Pfeffer, which she didn't like at all.

Anne, Margot and Peter van Pels carried on with their lessons while they were in hiding. They hoped they'd soon be back at school, and they didn't want to get behind.
Anne loved history, but she hated maths!

Peter was two-and-a-half years older than Anne. At first she thought he was boring.

As the months went by she changed her mind. Peter became Anne's special friend. For a while Anne even felt she was in love with him.

All this time, Anne carried on writing her diary.

She decided she wanted to be a writer when she grew up. As well as her diary, she began writing stories. She hoped one day they would be published.

The Franks, the van Pels and Mr Pfeffer lived in the Secret Annex for more than two years.

I shall call them 'Tales from the Secret Annex.'

Anne grew a lot, but it was very hard to get new clothes. She wrote in her diary that her vests were so small they didn't even cover her tummy!

Chapter 5

Several times while Anne and her family were in hiding, the offices downstairs were burgled. Each time, everyone in the Secret Annex was terrified that the burglars might find their hiding place and tell the Nazis. But nothing happened.

One day, though, the Nazis did find out
about the Secret Annex. No one knows for
sure who told them.

Anne and her family heard shouting
downstairs. It was the police. They had come
to take everyone in the Annex away.

Later, Miep went to the Annex. She found Anne's diary and stories scattered on the floor. She gathered them together and took them home.

She didn't read them. Instead she put them away in her desk, ready to give back to Anne when Anne came home after the war.

But Anne never did come home. She and her family were sent to Nazi concentration camps. There Anne died through lack of food, warmth and shelter.

In less than a year, Margot, Mrs Frank, Mr and Mrs van Pels, Peter and Mr Pfeffer had all died too.

The only person from the Annex to survive was Mr Frank. After the war, he found his way to Miep's home.

Miep gave Mr Frank Anne's diary and stories. He had never read them before.

Mr Frank let his friends read parts of Anne's diary too. They told him it was so good, he should have it published!

So in 1947, the first edition of Anne's diary went on sale. Her ambition to become a writer had come true, after all!

After the Story

Bestseller

Anne Frank is now more famous than she could ever have dreamt!

Her diary has been translated into over 60 languages, and more than 25 million copies have been sold.

Museum

The Secret Annex has become a museum, and today you can still go and see the rooms where Anne and her family hid, and where Anne wrote her diary. Visit the Anne Frank Museum website at: www.annefrank.org to find out more about Anne Frank.

Hiding

Lots of other Jews tried to hide from the Nazis. Some even lived under the floor boards of their houses! Many, though, like Anne and her family, were betrayed and taken away.

The Holocaust

Six million Jews and millions of other people were murdered between 1938 and 1945. This is known as the Holocaust. It was organised by the German Nazi Party.

Otto Frank

Otto Frank, the only one from the Annex to survive, lived until he was 91. He spent the rest of his life telling people, especially young people, about Anne's ideas. In spite of the war, Anne wrote about her belief in people's goodness and her hopes for peace.

Important dates in Anne Frank's lifetime

June 1929 Anne Frank is born in Frankfurt, Germany.

March 1933 Hitler becomes leader of Germany.

1933 Anne's family moves to Amsterdam, in the Netherlands.

1934 Anne goes to school.

1939 onwards The Germans round up Jews and other groups and take them to concentration camps.

September 1939 Germany invades Poland. Britain and France declare war on Germany.

1940–41 Germany invades Denmark, Norway, Belgium, the Netherlands, France, Greece, Yugoslavia and the Soviet Union.

1941 America and Canada join the war against Japan and Germany.

June 1942 Otto Frank gives his daughter, Anne, a diary for her birthday.

July 1942 The Frank family moves into the Secret Annex to hide from the Germans.

1943 onwards The war is changing. The Germans are not winning so many victories.

August 4, 1944 Police raid the Secret Annex and the Frank family are taken to concentration camps.

March 1945 Margot and Anne Frank die.

May 1945 Germany surrenders and war in Europe ends.

June 1945 Otto Frank returns to Amsterdam.

1947 The *Diary of Anne Frank* is published.

Quiz

Can you remember?

1. What country did Anne's family come from originally?

2. What was Anne's favourite present on her 13th birthday?

3. What were some of the things that Hitler would not let Jews do?

4. Who were Anne's family hiding from?

5. What did Anne do instead of packing a suitcase?

6. Where was the Secret Annex that Anne's family hid in?

7. How many people ended up hiding in the annex?

8. How long were they in hiding for?

9. Which member of the Frank family survived?

10. When did Anne's diary go on sale for the first time?

Answers on page 32.

Glossary

Annex Extra rooms or space added on to a building.

Burgled When someone breaks into a building and steals things.

Concentration camp A prison where a lot of people are kept together in horrible conditions.

Diary A book in which you write down what happens to you every day.

Hitler Adolf Hitler led the Nazi party in Germany.

Invade Enter a country to take over its rule.

Jewish Someone of the Jewish race or religion.

Nazi A member of the National Socialist Party in Germany which was led by Adolf Hitler.

Published To produce a document and sell it so that everyone can read it.

Index

Quiz answers

1. Germany
2. A diary
3. Have jobs, bicycles and cars, go out after 8pm
4. The Nazis
5. Wore lots of clothes on top of each other
6. In the building her father used to work in
7. 8
8. Over two years
9. Mr Otto Frank
10. 1947